NICENE CREED

Stephen C. Rowan

NICENE CREED

POETIC WORDS *for a* PROSAIC WORLD

XXIII
TWENTY-THIRD PUBLICATIONS
Mystic, Connecticut

A Note on Inclusive Language

At two points in the Nicene Creed the word "man" could be altered to show that it really includes women as well as men. Instead of saying, "for us men and for our salvation," the text could easily read, "for us and for our salvation." The Latin text says, "qui propter nos *homines*," which is the inclusive word for "humanity." Likewise, the words "he was born of the Virgin Mary and became man (*homo*)" could be changed to read "...and became human." However, because God is called "Father" and because Spirit is called "Lord," I have retained the use of the masculine pronoun in this book when referring to God.

Twenty-Third Publications
185 Willow Street
P.O. Box 180
Mystic, CT 06355
(203)536-2611

ISBN 0-89622-451-1
Library of Congress Catalog Number 90-70989

CONTENTS

THE NICENE CREED

We believe in one God,
the Father, the Almighty,
maker of heaven and earth,
of all that is seen and unseen.

We believe in one Lord, Jesus Christ,
the only Son of God,
eternally begotten of the Father,
God from God, Light from Light,
true God from true God,
begotten, not made, one in being with the Father.
Through him all things were made.
For us men and for our salvation
he came down from heaven:

by the power of the Holy Spirit
he was born of the Virgin Mary, and became man.

For our sake he was crucified under Pontius Pilate;
he suffered, died, and was buried.
On the third day he rose again
in fulfillment of the Scriptures;
he ascended into heaven
and is seated at the right hand of the Father.
He will come again in glory to judge the living and the dead,
and his kingdom will have no end.

We believe in the Holy Spirit, the Lord, the giver of life,
who proceeds from the Father and the Son.
With the Father and the Son he is worshiped and glorified.
He has spoken through the Prophets.
We believe in one holy catholic and apostolic Church.
We acknowledge one baptism for the forgiveness of sins.
We look for the resurrection of the dead,
and the life of the world to come. Amen.

INTRODUCTION

THE NICENE CREED, recited every Sunday at Mass, is a response of faith to the gospel. Composed by people whose first language was Greek or Latin, the Creed defined the Catholic faith in response to certain challenges against it. Although the challenges were local and temporary, people have continued to use these words for 1500 years because they express so well and so succinctly the core of the church's faith. However, precisely because of its age, its original language, and the obscure controversies that occasioned its composition, the Creed can sound strange or even "greek" to those who dutifully repeat it every Sunday.

My purpose, then, is to provide some understanding of the Creed, especially for beginners. I hope that catechumens exploring the Catholic faith through the Rite of Christian Initiation for Adults (R.C.I.A.) or young adults preparing for confirmation will find this introduction helpful, but I also have in mind anyone who has ever wondered what these words can mean or what difference they might make in day-to-day living or in our understanding of our faith.

Throughout this book I will be speaking of the Creed as a story and describing its words as "poetic." At the start, then, I want to explain what I mean by those terms so that it will be clear why I find them helpful for explaining the meaning of the Creed today.

To the casual ear, the Nicene Creed sounds like a series of propositions about one God called Father, one Lord Jesus Christ, and the Holy Spirit who is also called "Lord" and "giver of life." Where, one might ask, is the story line? Looked at very closely, however, the Creed does tell a story; there is a "flow" to the propositions or incidents whereby the narrative moves through a beginning, a middle, and an end.

To paraphrase the story briefly, we live in a world (a "heaven and an earth") which is also a "creation" (not a "chaos"); that is, from the beginning the world has a plan or a purpose given to it by its "Maker." Since that purpose is only dimly seen at best, Jesus is "sent" "for us and for our salvation" as the clear and trustworthy word to light up the path, in fact, to be the path itself through which we can find the way to God with firm assurance. Once he is "sent," Jesus is available to all, but unless he is understood to be the very word of God and unless he is accepted as such, his word will not produce any results. His mind must be understood as if from "within," in the same way that a friend's words are easily interpreted by the one who "instinctively" understands them. A person must somehow share in the "Spirit" of Christ in order to understand the mind of Christ. To some degree, all people can share in this Spirit because God wants all people to be saved and to come to a knowledge of the truth (see 1 Timothy 2:4). However, those who recognize explicitly that the Spirit of Jesus is the "giver of life" are united by that Spirit to Christ in a "communion of saints"; they live for "everlasting life" with a faith, a hope, and a love that are nourished and renewed by acts of forgiveness and communion.

This, then, is the story of each human life according to the Creed, a movement from what has been and already is to what will be: the life of the world to come. Each person is invited to see the actions of Father, Son, and Spirit in the work of creating, re-creating, and making ready the human person for life everlasting.

Although the story of each person is, in some sense, the same, it is also true that each story is unique because each person is made differently, is re-created in different ways, and is able to enjoy life everlasting according to different capacities for knowledge and love.

In its arrangement of words, the Creed tells a story; moreover, the words themselves are "poetic" in order to tell that story as effectively as possible. Unfortunately, in our culture something sounds less than serious if it is called poetic. However, unless it can be understood that the Creed is using words of a special kind for a special purpose, its message will be greatly misunderstood. "Poetic" words are not fancy or "high falutin'" words that might rhyme with one another or sound "pretty." This kind of language is more properly called "verse," a pleasing or at least rhythmic way of saying something, most often something sentimental, like the often parodied verse: "Roses are red, violets are blue/ Sugar is sweet and so are you."

Poetry, unlike verse, is a way of saying something that could not be said so well in any other way. As American poet Robert Frost has said, "Poetry is what gets lost in the translation." Poetic words are irreplaceable ways of saying something and saying it in such a way that along with the idea of the subject, something of its "mystery" is opened up. The poet, like a "seismograph," is sensitive to the "deep down things" of life. Once these reverberations of reality are picked up, the poet finds it necessary to use language with great exactness and intensity in order to etch out the experience.

Precisely because it is as exact as possible, poetic language can sound strange or "hard to grasp." In order to be exact, the poetic word must be subtle and necessarily indirect; it must convey a mystery that cannot be seen or heard directly. Like the squiggles of a seismograph, poetic words express something like an earthquake to people at a certain distance from the event. The "squiggles" are the so-called figures of speech: similes, metaphors, symbolic language, and paradox, for example. Because these figures do not name something directly, they preserve the mystery; at the same time, because they are indeed alluding to something, they communicate it to a certain extent. A person on the street might say, "My love is Susan"; the poet Robert Burns will say, "My love is like a red, red rose." Like the person on the street, the poet clearly means something, but means it indirectly.

In the following poem, for example, the poet Emily Dickinson writes of two experiences that are common enough, each throwing light on the other: a cat's stalking of a bird and a person's loss of a long-awaited hope that has lain temptingly just within grasp:

> She sights a bird—she chuckles—
> She flattens—then she crawls—
> She runs without the look of feet—
> Her eyes increase to Balls—
>
> Her Jaws stir—twitching—hungry—
> Her Teeth can hardly stand—
> She leaps, but Robin leaped the first—
> Ah, Pussy of the Sand,
>
> The Hope so juicy ripening—
> You almost bathed your Tongue—
> When Bliss disclosed a hundred Toes—
> And fled with every one—

Now, although the experiences of a cat stalking a bird and a person tracking down hope are common enough, the poet helps a person to recognize their significance and to feel the bitter disappointment when the enterprise fails. The poet conveys the mystery of the human condition, using for this purpose words that sometimes give at best only an indirect account of what is taking place. In no way, for example, are the cat's eyes really "balls" nor do birds literally have "toes," much less a hundred of them.

To put it another way, you could not put this scene on a videotape exactly as Dickinson describes it; it could not be verified by any of the senses, and yet the truth of the scene comes through. What the poet wants to say is expressed, even if it must be by the indirect language of symbol, exaggeration, and metaphor. It is only by patiently following these indirect signs that a reader finds the poet's directions out.

If poetic words are needed to express the mystery of everyday experience, they are needed even more to express the mystery of God. Since no one has ever seen God, any experience of God must necessarily be indirect, and in order to communicate the experience adequately, the words about it must be indirect as well.

Consider the traveler who tries to convey the gist of an experience to those who have remained at home. He may try a literal account for awhile, but these words are not the experience itself, and, besides, the experience was something both sensed and felt by the whole person, a complex of impressions that could not be caught on film or in a literal account. Eventually, as the emotion builds or as frustration mounts, the traveler finds himself using comparisons and saying what it was like to see the sight. Soon enough, however, he ends up saying, "You've just got to see it for yourself." The experience amounts to much more than what he saw or what he could say about it, and so he preserves the mystery with respectful silence after having made every effort to tell it all.

Likewise, the words of the Creed are the church's way of telling what she knows of God insofar as God can be known by the testimony of the Scriptures and the use of human reason. The Creed is a translation of those travelers' reports known as the four gospels and the other Scriptures by someone who has a living sense of what the travelers have seen and are trying to say. The translation is "poetic" and not literal in order to come as close as possible to the truth of the experience, a dimension of life that must always remain to some extent mysterious.

In the Creed, the church will say that God is a "Maker," even though literally speaking God has no hands and no tools. The church will say that Jesus "came down" from heaven, even though the discoveries of science seem to show that heaven is not literally "up," and the church will say that God is a holy "spirit" (or breath), even though God has no material substance, not even a substance as thin as the air.

Finally, we can call the words of the Creed poetic because the poetic word has power to unite each person who hears the word with all the others who hear it. For the language of everyday life, the intended audience of a communication is usually specific and narrow. For example, a phone call, a business memo, or a shopping list is not meant to be shared with the public at large. However, the poet's word is meant for all who will identify with it and apply it to themselves. So, Emily Dickinson's cat is at the same time both a particular cat and a way of speaking about the pursuit of happiness which applies more to people than to cats and which many people can recognize as their own pursuit.

It is strangely true that the particular, irreplaceable poetic word has the power to convey a universal message; that the single, particular image invites many people to identify with it. In the words of Archibald MacLeish, the poet provides "for all the history of grief, an empty doorway and a maple leaf." And so to call the Creed poetic is to claim for it the power to reach many people of many times and places with a message that is truly ecumenical. The Creed tells the story of God in such a way that in the particular actions of creating, saving, and making holy, people can identify a pattern that makes sense of their own lives. "This is, indeed, what God is doing," they might say, and by saying this they recognize their fellowship with all who have ever said the same thing.

In the chapters that follow, I take selected words from the several articles of the Creed and examine them as figurative speech that communicates probative insight. I hope that those who reflect on these words with me will come to see how wise they are, how deeply they penetrate the mystery of life, even to the marrow of it, where nourishing purpose and meaning are to be found.

Questions for Reflection and Discussion

1. As you reflect on an important event in your life (for example, your first interview for a job or a fight you had with a parent or spouse), which details or incidents do you include and which ones would you leave out when you tell a story about the event? Why do you make the choices you do? Why, do you think, is a story necessary for remembering the event? As you answer these questions, try to see the difference between an *event* that includes "whatever is going on" and the *story* which is a *selection* of incidents for the sake of making a point or of sharpening perception into an event.

2. In the poem by Emily Dickinson quoted in the introduction, assess the poet's choice of words. What does she gain, for example, by saying that the cat "chuckles" or that she is "Pussy of the Sand"? What does she gain by her use of exaggeration? How effectively does the cat-bird comparison throw light on the human situation? What difference would there be if some word were substituted for another in the text or if, for example, Dickinson had written of a dog chasing a cat instead of a cat chasing a bird?

3. If poetry is not valued highly as "serious" language in our culture, how do you account for this? To what extent is it necessary to talk about God in poetic language? Can you find a way of talking about God that excludes any use of poetry?

4. Take one of your favorite stories from the gospels. To what extent are its words poetic in the ways described in this chapter?

5. In his essay, "Poetry and the Christian," Karl Rahner claims that unless a person has an ear for the poetic word, that person cannot be Christian. What might Rahner mean by this? To what extent is his claim true?

PART ONE

We believe in one God
the Father, the Almighty,
maker of heaven and earth,
of all that is seen and unseen.

FROM ITS FIRST WORDS, the Creed makes clear that it is an act of faith, and to some people this alone disqualifies it from serious attention. Our culture, in the main, values "raw data" (which it equates with the only knowledge "worth having") and is, at best, tolerant of beliefs as long as they remain merely personal opinions. "Well, if that's what you believe..." is one way to end a discussion that cannot be decided by a look at the graphs, the statistics, or the color of the solution in the test tube.

Yet some of the most important decisions that we make follow from what we can only believe to be true for us. Only with belief can a person answer such questions as: Should I marry or not? If I do, should it be this person or someone else? Should we have children? If so, how do we raise them? Should I work at a certain job or profession, and develop one or another of my talents?

Beyond the personal realm, we believe that certain policies are good for the nation and, in the broadest context, that life is worth living and that it has a certain purpose. All of the human knowledge that can be tested to be true is only the tip of the iceberg; what we imagine and trust to be true lies, we know, much deeper.

Of course, we like to appear that we know what we're doing. We like the control that comes from knowing the facts and predicting what follows from them. But if we are honest we will admit that many of our decisions are made without having any clearly established facts to guide us. We are aware that even the best of what we know is a risk, a trusting that something is so or is for the best.

Christian faith is an especially risky act of trust because it wagers that there is a steady, final purpose to who we are as persons, that all of our acts of knowing and loving have as their implicit and final object what we call "God," and that with God as their object, these acts and we ourselves have meaning. Trusting in God is risky because it is done despite arguments and evidence to the contrary. Some people trust in God, for example, because they see evidence of order in the world; they are convinced, too, that this order can be known to some extent because the world seems to be put together in such a way that it is knowable in the first place. We find that we can check one fact or theory against another and grow in knowledge by discounting what is false and keeping what is true. We can change theories and move from truth to truth without losing a sense of coherence only because there seems to be a standard of truth in light of which all truths are seen to be only more or less adequate expressions. "God," to this way of thinking, is shorthand for the Truth that lies beyond and in between the lines of any one truth, giving it stable grounding and relative importance. God—or Being itself—is what we strive to know when we seek to know any one being, however humble. This is what the poet was suggesting when he wrote:

> To see a world in a grain of sand
> > And a Heaven in a Wild Flower,
> Hold Infinity in the palm of your hand,
> > And Eternity in an hour.

Now, while it makes sense to trust that God exists based on the evidence of an order we seem made to know, it is also true that there is evidence of disorder or of seemingly random events. The philosopher Voltaire, for example, could not accept any arguments for a well-constructed universe in the aftermath of an earthquake in 1755 that destroyed the city of Lisbon, Portugal, killing thousands of its inhabitants. Every age has its own examples of seemingly random or unplanned events: from monstrous hurricanes, earthquakes, and volcanic eruptions to genetic leaps up the ladder of evolution. In our time, we are more conscious of such seemingly freak occurrences because improvements in communication make them known almost as soon as they happen.

To trust, then, that we are made to know God is to trust in a stable truth that endures despite evidence to the contrary and to take the risk that one may be deceived. The risk would not be such a heavy penalty to pay in itself, except that believing in God brings with it a commitment to look for the truth and to respect it wherever it is found. This entails inconveniences unknown to those who assume that there is no God or truth, that they can make up their reality as they go along (and that therefore they are free to do whatever they please), that everything is permitted because nothing matters much one way or the other.

To speak scornfully of those who seem to need the "consolations" of religion (namely, a comforting assurance that God is in his heaven and all is right with the world) is to know very little about what a struggle it is to believe in the first place and especially how unconsoling it is to believe that one must be true to God—to what is really there—and not cling to what is only wishful thinking.

If the act of faith is risky, it is not mindless. It is a kind of reason that Cardinal Newman called the "illative sense." This is the faculty of mind that concludes what is "there" (*illa*) after pondering the probable opinions concerning the matter at hand. For example, from a certain point of view there is evidence of disorder in creation from the growth of cancer cells to the eruptions of a volcano. However, there is also evidence of order from the growth of a fertilized egg into the walking wonder of a child to the regularity of the speed of light. With evidence of both kinds, the mind ponders what is more probably the case: that we live in a chaotic world that only seems to be orderly at times, or that we live in a seemingly chaotic world whose order we cannot fully comprehend.

It is probable that certain facts of human life—unless they are absurd—point to the presence of some kind of meaning or purpose: like hope for life that endures despite the fact of death, like the roar of laughter that judges something to be absurd or beside the point; like the tug of conscience that opposes an injustice that exists for the sake of a justice that does not yet exist. These traits of human nature infer some kind of purpose, and, as I picture it, they converge with the absurdities of life like so many rays of light toward a cloud behind which they disappear. Faith, as the illative sense, risks the judgment that behind the cloud is a source of light that would explain everything that emanates from it. Thanks to God, in other words, a person has reason to trust that all truths, including the truths to be found in everyday acts of knowledge and decision making, are grounded in truth itself. For that reason, striving to know and to choose rightly is for real; it counts, it matters, it makes a real difference to one's being alive.

To say, then, that we believe in God is to take a step full of risk down a road where one trusts to find the truth in every act of knowing, a truth that will exhaust a person's search for it long before it can ever be exhausted itself.

FATHER

Christians believe in God who is the truth sought in every act of knowing, who is the good yearned for in every act of loving, who is as close to us as the workings of the mind and heart. Besides trusting that God exists, Christian faith trusts further that God reveals himself both implicitly and explicitly: *implicitly* in the way the world "works," in the structures that are discovered through the many scientific and humanistic ways of knowing, and *explicitly* in the stories of a people found in the Bible, which records both the experiences of these people and their interpretations of that experience. Christian faith considers these stories "inspired," at least in the sense that through them one can "hear" with authority the intentions that God has for humanity.

These intentions of God are mediated through the human authors of the books of the Bible; consequently, the writings, or "Scriptures," must be interpreted with intelligence, that is, we should understand what they reveal to us in and through the way they "work" as texts. Since the meaning of a text is not always as obvious as it seems, it takes the effort of critical attention to understand what kind of story we are reading and how to interpret what is read. Even so, the God of the Bible is revealed more clearly—is a more tangible character in the course of a story—than the God known only through the reflections of reason.

If "we believe" in the God who is the hero of the Bible, we do so with all of the risk of faith but with very good reason: we can see that this God and these stories make sense of our lives. They pass the pragmatic test of giving direction to that intricate maze which is the human heart. Drawing its inspiration from the Scriptures, then, the Creed begins with the Christian belief that God is "Father." This is to use a poetic way of speaking not only found in the Jewish Scriptures but also favored by Jesus himself.

As with all metaphors, the word as it is found in the Bible is deflected from a literal, descriptive purpose and is placed in a literary context—usually a story—where its meaning has to be discovered by inferences drawn from that context. In responding to the biblical story, a reader's personal experience with a biological father will be only more or less helpful. In fact, a person's private associations could distort the biblical meaning as surely as they could help to interpret it. Therefore, the more thoroughly a reader notices the particular events of the story and the meaning that emerges from the context, the more richly revealing the term "father" will be.

In the Bible, God is called "father" primarily because of the parent-like ties to his people, or "children." Because the bonding between parents and offspring creates a strong and natural motive for attention and care, the biblical writers use it to describe God's care for the people of Israel, especially in his leading them out of Egypt into the land of promise where they will be free and a people fully themselves. According to the prophet Hosea (11:1–4), God is like a parent who has undertaken the sometimes frustrating project of raising a child. With special tenderness, God says:

When Israel was a child I loved him,
     Out of Egypt I called my son.
The more I called them,
     The farther they went from me....
Yet it was I who taught Ephraim to walk,

who took them in my arms;
I drew them with human cords,
  with bands of love;
I fostered them like one
  who raises an infant to his cheeks;
Yet, though I stooped to feed my child,
  they did not know that I was their healer.

It also happens that God is called a mother in the Bible. Because mothers are known the world over for their tender love, Isaiah the prophet (49:15) is moved to compare this love to God's own tender but fierce devotion:

Can a mother forget her infant,
  be without tenderness for the child of her womb?
Even should she forget,
  I will never forget you.

However, in the Bible "father" is used more often when speaking of God perhaps because in the culture addressed by the biblical authors the father enjoyed special rights and duties—even a certain dominance—within the family. As the example from Hosea shows, fathers can be capable of quite tender affection, but at some point they may also be called to lay down the law. In the biblical world, it seems that "father" signifies not only an accepting love but a challenging love as well. Perhaps this is partly because even in a physical way fathers can get only so close to their children. They can meet cheek to cheek, as Hosea says, but men's breasts don't work. For that reason, fathers more aptly provide a love that calls the child just beyond the present moment, invites the child to make always more progress, and urges the child to grow to full stature.

When God is called "the father of orphans and the defender of widows" (Psalm 68:6), it is not only because God is the "parent" who "gives a home to the forsaken" but also because God "leads forth prisoners to prosperity." As "father," God takes responsibility for and an active interest in the people; he nourishes them and provides a home for them, but the suggestion persists that God wants them to go farther and to become even more than they are.

Also, without forgetting to show mercy, God reminds the people of his "covenant" with them, the way of life they have promised to keep, precisely so that they will know how to find the path to real life. God is compassionate "as a father has compassion on his children" because he "knows how we are formed; he remembers that we are dust"; we are "only human," in other words. And yet God does not deny justice—the truth of who God is and what follows from that—because he can be known and enjoyed only by "those who keep the covenant and remember to fulfill his precepts" (Psalm 103:16-19).

Because the Bible's authors know that freedom is always for the sake of obtaining some good—some promised land, for example—they show gratitude for God's father-like giving of the law; it is a light on the path, a way to find life, not a hampering of life. Freedom from Egypt would mean nothing if it meant just wandering aimlessly in the desert; freedom must always be for the good that lies ahead.

In the New Testament, Jesus himself draws on this Jewish experience of God and reenforces it. For him, God is "Abba," a particularly intimate Aramaic word for "father." St. Mark records (14:36) that Jesus uses this word in his moment of trial in the garden on the night before he died: "Abba, Father, all things are possible to you. Take this cup away from me, but not what I will but what you will." It seems that when he needs to show trust in God at the moment of maximum danger, Jesus can find no word more suitable to his purpose than "Abba."

The word Jesus used must have been widely remembered as revealing the very mind of Christ, because St. Paul says that when we cry out "Abba, Father," we show that the very Spirit of God's son has been sent into our hearts (Galatians 4:16). Because Jesus himself had this intimate relationship with God, the first words he taught his disciples to pray were the very secret of his closeness: they were to call God "our Father." And, when you think about it, Jesus showed us great mercy when he agreed to tell his disciples what it was that he said to his father when he was alone.

Implied in the word "father" is the idea that God is personal, that is, something more like a person than not, with purposes and intentions toward humanity. This makes possible some kind of identification with God, but at the same time creates problems for the imagination and the mind.

For example, to say that God is a person encourages the imagination to picture God as one being among others. Encouraged by images drawn from the Bible, the imagination might want to picture an old man with a white beard (the "ancient of days") or something like the Roman god Jupiter with his supply of lightning bolts. In time, these images become so commonplace that the holy, awesome God becomes a subject for cartoons and stale jokes. Even if God could be pictured as the most exalted of beings, it limits God to imply that he is only one being among others. So, by the principle of analogy, God is understood to be both personal and not a person in the human sense.

There is also a danger that calling God "father" can imply that God has a sex, though the Bible does not take God's sex any way into account as the mythologies of other religions do. There is no story about God as there is about Jupiter, for example, who sought maids to mate with and a wife to marry. God is "father" for the purpose of saying many things, but privileging one sex over another is not one of them. God is called father by analogy with human fathers of a particular culture for the sake of saying several things about God, mostly about his love shown in provident care. Other associations are beside the point.

MAKER OF HEAVEN AND EARTH

Along with "provident father," God is called the "maker of heaven and earth." This analogy suggests a craftsperson of some kind, specifically a potter in one or two contexts. The second account of creation (Genesis 2:4–3:24) is especially graphic in its use of this metaphor, telling as it does of God's kneading the Adam (dust) from the dust of the earth and breathing into him a breath of life. Reading the "how" of creation literally would land a person in several difficulties, the first of which is that it contradicts the "how" of the first account of creation in Genesis 1:1–2:4, where God's word alone and not his hands establishes everything in its place: "God said, 'Let there be light,' and there was light" (Genesis 1:3). But the second difficulty would be just as real: to picture God with hands and so to make God once again only one being among others.

As with "father," the word "maker" needs to be interpreted by teasing out the implications of the metaphor in its context. Two meanings seem to be that a maker has a purpose for a product and has rights over it. God as "maker" of heaven and earth is pictured, then, as someone working with a design in mind, trying to shape some rude materials into something remarkable. Furthermore, as the only one who knows the design he has in mind, he alone has the right to say whether this particular creation has come up to his idea of it or not.

"Father" and "maker" are ways of saying that one's life has a plan and that by providing the plan God gives us more than we can ever give ourselves. Living within the mystery of that provident care, our lives are a reason for gratitude.

ALMIGHTY

With the word "almighty," the Creed expresses confidence that the plan of God will hold, that it cannot be replaced or thwarted by any force whatever. If, as the letter to the Ephesians says (1:3), "God chose us in [Christ] before the foundation of the world to be holy and without blemish," if "in love he destined us for adoption to himself through Jesus Christ," then this remains the plan and nothing can change it. God's power to keep a promise is as sure as the mercy with which the promise was made in the first place.

"Almighty" will be misunderstood if it is taken to mean that God meddles arbitrarily in the world and shows power in such a way that people are compelled to yield to it. Unlike Jupiter, God is not given to throwing around thunderbolts just to make people shape up. As a matter of fact, thunder and lightning may suggest the awesomeness of God but in themselves are merely forces of nature. Only when they are coupled through the story with a revelation of God's intentions (as in the book of Exodus 19:16–19, for example) do such forces work as part of God's plan: they draw attention to the awesomeness of the words of God that must be heard—and then accepted—if one is to find life.

Even the miracles of Jesus in the gospels are not arbitrary acts of power; rather, they are "visual aids" of the good news, showing in graphic terms what Jesus means when he says, "The kingdom of God is among you" (Luke 17:21). The kingdom means health—total health—of which the faculties of sight, speech, and upright walking are apt enough symbols. Also, the miracles are linked with the need to have faith; as Matthew says (13:58), Jesus could not work many "mighty deeds" in Nazareth, his home town, because of the people's "lack of faith." In other words, people must freely accept what God is showing them in these deeds. God is almighty in the sense that his plan remains firm and will not be thwarted; it will come to pass for those who co-operate with it. But the plan can be rejected. God's power stops just short of forcing human freedom because God is also powerful enough to let that freedom be, taking the risk that people will use that freedom wisely and will cooperate with the plan: to be "holy" and so find "life."

As we have seen, there are many reasons to doubt that the plan will hold or that there is even a plan at all. There are many apparent "kinks" in creation, evidence that the world is less than perfect according to human standards. For many people, this has argued against God's power. If God were all-powerful, they say, he would work the kinks out—now.

However, Christians can say with confidence that there is a plan—despite evidence of physical and moral evils ("kinks") in the world—because they have learned the mystery of the cross, which says that what the world judged to be weakness turned out to be strength and what the world judged to be foolishness turned out to be wisdom. The cross of Christ looked like defeat but was really victory. It was, as St. John puts it, a "lifting up," a lifting up of the cross into the place of execution and a lifting up of Jesus as a sign of victory for all the world to see. Once the church witnessed the plan of God in all its fullness, it learned the wisdom of Jesus' prayer of trust: "Father, into your hands, I commend my Spirit." Even Calvary, it seems, could not defeat the plan of God to reconcile everything in heaven and on earth and "to make peace by the blood of [the] cross" (Colossians 1:20).

To say that "we believe in one God, the Father, the Almighty, Maker of heaven and earth" is to say that we believe in a loving plan for creation that will hold despite the many threats against it. And so the story begins with a promise of purpose within a world where it is possible to learn that purpose and to cooperate with it. To learn about the plan itself, we must continue the story and understand what it means to say, "We believe in one Lord, Jesus Christ."

QUESTIONS FOR REFLECTION AND DISCUSSION

1. Do you have a sense that your life has a purpose? If you do, what is its purpose and how do you know it?

2. What experiences give you confidence that there is a God?

3. What do you mean by "God"?

4. To what extent is the comparison of God with "father" helpful to you?

5. What images of God appeal to you? Why? What stories about God do you like?

6. If you were to learn for certain that God did or did not exist, what difference would that make in your life?

7. What makes it difficult to believe in God, or what makes it easy to forget God, in the way we live our lives in this country at this time?

PART TWO

We believe in one Lord, Jesus Christ,
  the only Son of God,
  eternally begotten of the Father,
  God from God, Light from Light,
  true God from true God,
  begotten, not made, one in being with the Father.
  Through him all things were made.
  For us men and for our salvation
    he came down from heaven:

by the power of the Holy Spirit
  he was born of the Virgin Mary, and became man.

For our sake he was crucified under Pontius Pilate;
  he suffered, died, and was buried.
  On the third day he rose again
    in fulfillment of the Scriptures;
  he ascended into heaven
    and is seated at the right hand of the Father.
He will come again in glory to judge
  the living and the dead,
  and his kingdom will have no end.

IN MANY WAYS, Jesus of Nazareth has captured the imagination of millions of people. In the West, the present year is dated from the supposed year of his birth, as if to say that something happened at that time that has made all the difference down the years. What happened—or at least the several versions of what happened—is contained in the three words: "Jesus," "Christ," and "Lord." The man Jesus, born of a woman in a particular time and place, is also a person set aside or anointed for a mission (the word "Christ" is from the Greek word meaning "anointed"), which reveals him as Lord of a people, worthy of their allegiance and capable of bringing them the good that God has promised: "peace" and "salvation."

By the time the story of Jesus is set down in the gospels, decades of reflection have interpreted what he meant to his first companions so that belief in Jesus rests not on what he says of himself but on what others have said of him. At the same time, the "news" is always the testimony of believers so that it is impossible to strip away the layers of interpretation completely and to see the uninsulated Jesus. Some scholars have succeeded in recovering some sense of the "very words" of Jesus and an idea of what he truly did, but in the end each person is left with the testimony in the New Testament. Each person is attracted to one image or story of Jesus more than another, while recognizing that each perspective can be enriched by another.

For example, Jesus is "good shepherd" but also "lamb of God"; the one who seeks out the rich tax collector, Zaccheus, but who also expels the money changers from the temple; Jesus sows his word as a sower of seed, catches disciples as he catches fish, and gathers children into his arms. Jesus promises to come as a thief in the night or as a bridegroom to his bride. The Creed does not adjudicate the adequacy of these different images of Jesus. Much less does it oblige us to prefer one over the other. Rather, the Creed simply affirms that the belief of Christians is in Jesus, in someone who really walked the earth.

It is clear that the four gospel writers, the apostle Paul, and the other New Testament writers have learned something different from this Jesus and yet whatever they have learned has been gleaned from the same person. This is a momentous thought: whatever we know of God as Christians we know through Jesus, and, even more accurately, through what others have said of him. At the heart of Catholic belief is the "sacramental" principal that the knowledge and love of God are mediated to us. "No one has ever seen God," says St. John in his gospel, who then adds immediately, "The only Son, God, who is at the Father's side, has revealed him" (1:18).

To believe in Jesus is to believe that his humanity sheds light not only on God but on our own humanity. After all, if we learn of God through human life, then anything we know of what it means to be human will allow us to grasp fully the story of Jesus. The gospels are highly selective in what they say of Jesus (they never describe his physical appearance, for example), and the Creed is even more selective. But both the gospels and the Creed agree that the importance of Jesus lies in the fact that he is the Christ, the man with a mission: to teach with authority.

In the words of the Creed, Jesus is the one "through whom all things were made." Recalling the image of God as a maker with a purpose, this phrase suggests that it is Jesus whom the Father kept in mind to guide him in his making of the world—just as a craftsman uses a design to remind him of his desired goal.

Jesus is the "Wisdom" as well as the "Word" of God, showing us in his flesh what God intends for us. That is why the church focuses its attention so closely on Jesus: he is the "new Adam," the *typical* human who shows us what things God has prepared for those who love him precisely because his humanity is truly our humanity. Jesus teaches this not only in what he says but even more in what he does. His message is not just a moral one ("If you keep my commandments, you will remain in my love" [John 15:10]) but an existential one as well ("Where I *am* there also will my servant be" [John 12:26]).

FOR US AND FOR OUR SALVATION, HE CAME DOWN FROM HEAVEN

What Jesus teaches is "for us and for our salvation"; it seems, however, that for most people salvation is not of obvious interest. More pressing needs are always at hand, requiring the management of time, income, and the resources of mind, emotions, and energy. The saving and spending of tangible goods necessarily occupy the forefront of most people's attention, not the saving of self. Salvation, then, can seem esoteric, the kind of word that does not fit easily into the idiom we use for real, everyday needs.

The irony, however, is that salvation addresses the most fundamental human need of all—a need so much at the core of a person that it can go undetected unless consciously attended to. The word salvation (from the Latin *salus*) refers to the "health" of a person in the most complete sense of the word, a health that can be maintained even in the face of the deadliest diseases and threats to life. It expresses the ability to stand whole and entire in the face of dreadful questions such as "Do I matter?" "Does my life have a purpose?" "If I misuse that purpose, can I recover it, or am I lost for good?"

Since the story of Jesus is told in the Scriptures and in the Creed "for us and for our salvation," it is told in a necessarily charged and poetic way in order to respect the unusual depth of its message. Much can be gained by seeing what is said and how it is arranged. From the gospel accounts of Matthew, Mark, Luke, and John, the Creed makes merely the barest outline of the life of Jesus; for example, there are no teachings recorded, no miracles named. Then the events are arranged in such a way that they make a perfect circle of coming down and of going up—from a lowering of the self to an exaltation of the self. Jesus is "one in being with the Father"; then, in a descending action, "comes down" from heaven, suffers, dies, and is buried, and then with an ascending action reverses the trajectory of his story and rises, ascends into heaven, and sits at the right hand of the Father.

This cyclic pattern is made clear in the earliest hymns of the Christian liturgy, such as the one Paul records in his letter to the Philippians (2:5–11):

Have among yourselves the same attitude
that is also yours in Christ Jesus,
Who, though he was in the form of God,
did not regard equality with God something to be grasped.
Rather, he emptied himself,
taking the form of a slave,
coming in human likeness;
and found human in appearance,
he humbled himself,
becoming obedient to death,
even death on a cross.
Because of this, God greatly exalted him
and bestowed on him the name
that is above every name,
that at the name of Jesus
every knee should bend,
of those in heaven and on earth and under the earth,
and every tongue confess that
Jesus is Lord,
to the glory of God the Father.

Such shaping of the story of Jesus shows more sharply not only what "took place" in his life but also, more importantly, what was "going on" in his life, what it meant: Jesus brought heaven to earth and earth to heaven in such a way that he made a permanent bonding or "at-one-ment" of the two worlds or dimensions of life. In doing this, Jesus answers in a saving way the awesome questions in people's hearts: "Do I matter?" Yes: "You are worth more than many sparrows" (Matthew 10:31). "Does my life have a purpose?" Yes: "Now this is eternal life, that they should know you, the only true God, and the one whom you sent, Jesus Christ"

(John 17:3). "If I neglect that purpose, can I recover it?" Yes: "Peace I leave with you; my peace I give to you" (John 14:27).

A story that is so shaped and carries such a message is sometimes called a "myth," which, as I use the term, is *not* at odds with "truth"; in fact, mythic language seeks to bring out what is really true, or the deepest truths, in what would otherwise appear to be normal, everyday events. Myth and meaning go together, not myth and misrepresentation. Mythic language may seem untrue only when people take it to be descriptive language and try to understand it as if it were a literal description of what was supposed to be happening in everyday life. In the clash that follows between a mythic account and a "common sense" description, it is not surprising that "common sense" most often wins. After all, everyone can see "what is taking place": the event as grasped by the senses; not everyone can agree about "what is going on": the meaning of the event grasped by faith.

For example, it is hard to picture Jesus literally coming down from heaven. The literal minded might well ask, "Where is heaven?" or, If heaven is "up there" somewhere, how does Jesus "come down"? The imagination boggles if it tries to supply a literal answer that would satisfy common sense.

So it helps to remember that the words are mythic: they signify what is at the level of deepest meaning, what concerns our salvation. To say, then, that the Lord Jesus "came down from heaven" is a way of saying that he speaks of the heavenly world with authority; he talks like an ambassador from the Father or like "one sent," as John's gospel describes him.

The first witnesses experienced Jesus as God's own word come among them; they recognized that the "origin" or source of what he said was not human but divine. To say that "the one who was sent came down from heaven" is to put into story form how the faith of those who experienced Jesus firsthand understood the event. Geographical terms are used to speak about moral and existential realities.

Philosophers and theologians may speak of heaven as a "dimension" or ground of experience: always there and always able to be tapped into. But a poet who has a story to tell will speak of heaven as a place of origin and a destination; heaven is the beginning and the end of Jesus' story as if to show by this circular pattern the complete, unchanging significance of who he is. And heaven is said to be "up" rather than "down" because of the tendency to "look up" to what is "elevating" or "exalted" and therefore more important, more impressive, more glorious. If heaven were literally up, that is where Jesus would be coming from. But the sense of the story is not that Jesus comes physically from any one direction but that, instead, he comes *as if* he were an ambassador from a distant place and speaks with authority about its promises and demands.

The Creed, then, shapes the story of Jesus in such a way that the heavenly dimension of his message and his person becomes more obvious. He came down from heaven is as much to the point of what we need to know for our salvation as the fact that he was truly born of a woman. And, for that matter, the fact that Mary is a "virgin" is as much to the point of the story as the fact that she is a mother.

BORN OF THE VIRGIN MARY

Mary's perpetual virginity, literally understood, has often been questioned partly because this would seem to require a miracle, a suspension of the natural order of things, and belief in miracles has always been hard to come by, and partly because Mark's gospel speaks of Jesus' "brothers" (3:31), which suggests to some that Mary had other children. In general, Protestants tend to deemphasize Mary in contrast to Catholics who revere her with an especially intense devotion. At one extreme, Protestants have been accused of seriously underestimating Mary's role; at the other extreme, Catholics have been denounced for adoring her. Since the evidence of the Scriptures is contested, it would be helpful to suspend the question of Mary's literal virginity at least long enough to ask Protestants, "Why do the Scriptures state so clearly that Mary is, indeed, a virgin (Matthew 2:18, Luke 1:27)?" and to ask Catholics, "Granting that Mary is a virgin, what difference does it make to say so?"

The answers to these questions lie in the symbolic suggestiveness of virginity. The first suggestion is that the birth of Jesus is pure grace, owing nothing to human initiative but everything to human cooperation. It is not Joseph's decision to have a baby—or even Mary's, for that matter—that brings about the birth of Jesus. Rather, the initiative is entirely God's as it was with the Jewish matriarchs: Sarah, the mother of Isaac; Manoah's wife, the mother of Samson; and Hannah, the mother of Samuel. The gospels of Matthew and Luke echo a motif from the Jewish Scriptures: the birth of Jesus is pure grace, not the result of human effort.

As if to stress that God's ways can often be indirect and even tainted with scandal, Matthew includes in Jesus' genealogy the reminder that the family tree back to Abraham includes not only kings and patriarchs but some unexpected ancestors: a woman who posed as a prostitute in order to have sexual relations with her father-in-law (Tamar), another who was a harlot (Rahab), one who was a foreigner (Ruth), and one who was the wife of another man when David took her to bed (Bathsheba). The list suggests, then, that the virgin birth is only one example of God's ability to take the most improbable of directions and to surprise people only in order to delight them in the end.

Mary's virginity suggests, as well, the fertile ground of a new creation. She is like the garden of Eden that stood as an oasis on the barren earth and provided a fit place for the innocent life of the man and the woman. In fact, Mary's obedient response to God has often suggested to many people a sharp contrast to the disobedience of Eve and Adam. In the suggestive language of symbol, Mary is at once a new garden of innocence and the woman who is set there to be the "mother of all the living" (Genesis 3:20) through a radical cooperation with God.

At all times, reverence for Mary increases in proportion to how well her role as virgin and mother is understood. As virgin, she cooperates fully with God and lets his will for her happen; as mother, she brings to birth and nourishes the new covenant who is Jesus. So, in her person, Mary unites a most powerful message: that God is both with us and for us in Jesus. At the same time, God tells us through Jesus that he is the Lord of history, able to take it on his own initiative in surprising directions.

As virgin and mother, Mary is an awesome and comforting figure, a wonderful mediation of the "holy" who arouses feelings both of salutary fear and fascination. The Catholic devotion to her stems in part from her ability to mediate the mystery of Jesus as both God and human.

All this being said, however, the Creed's primary emphasis is that Jesus was *born* of the virgin. As St. Paul told the Galatians (4:4), Jesus was "born of a woman," implying that Jesus is truly human, able to reveal in human terms "the things God has prepared for those who love him" (1 Corinthians 2:9). By insisting on the true humanity of Jesus, Paul claims the story of Jesus as a truly human story, showing Jesus to be the "first" of many brothers and sisters or, to change the metaphor, a human head of a human body (Ephesians 1:22). As the "firstborn" or as the "head," Jesus is the way who shows what follows "for us and for our salvation."

The principle is constantly stated in the writings of the early fathers of the church that if Jesus were not human, then humanity has not really been redeemed. The sense that humanity is truly a new creation in Christ (and not just imputed to be such)—that Jesus is a "second Adam," giving all who are "in him" a means to be truly free for God—can only follow from the fact that Jesus is truly human. So, in the Creed it is affirmed that Jesus was born of a woman, against all who would say that he hardly knew the human condition, that his body was only a shimmering appearance, that he hardly touched the earth in the flesh. These opinions are not common now, at least they are not so openly stated, but they have, indeed, been said before and they have challenged the church to state its belief clearly: Jesus is not only "true God from true God," but is also *"born* of the Virgin Mary."

He Suffered, Died, and was Buried

The words "he was crucified under Pontius Pilate, suffered, died, and was buried" bring Jesus to the low point of his story, the point of his apparent defeat. As we saw, Paul's letter to the Philippians identifies the death of Jesus on the cross with the depths of his humility, and he links the humility with the emptying it took to become human. The message, then, is clear: Jesus knows the human condition in its full spectrum, from cradle to grave. He is one with us on our entire journey. This is important because it means that whatever Jesus came to show us about the heavenly kingdom applies to us as we really are.

The gospel writers elaborate at greater length on the significance of Jesus' suffering and death. As they tell their stories, the cross contradicts those who have judged Jesus to be a criminal. Pontius Pilate wrote the inscription over the cross as a taunt to a subject people: "This is Jesus of Nazareth, King of the Jews" (John 19:19). He would have the world believe that Jesus was a rebel to Rome, a would-be king of the Jews. And yet the words are ironically true; Jesus is a king in a sense that seems to have escaped the Roman governor.

Each of the evangelists contributes something of his own emphasis to the meaning of this death. For Mark, it is an ugly death, as Jesus cries out the first verse of Psalm 22, "My God, My God, why have you forsaken me?" and breathes his last (15:33–37). And yet through this ugliness a certain truth can be seen by a Roman centurion: "Truly, this man was the Son of God!" (15:39).

Matthew presents a more exalted picture of the crucifixion, saying that Jesus "gave up his spirit" as if conscious of the sacrificial nature of his death, and describing a shaking of the earth as if in apocalyptic fury (27:50–51). Luke's account is more gentle and commanding, showing Jesus on the cross as he appeared to be in life: the giver of great pardons, a person of prayer, and the perfect witness for the kingdom. After Jesus forgives his enemies, saying "they know not what they do" (23:34), and after promising new life in his kingdom to a common criminal with the words "Today you will be with me in Paradise" (23:43), Jesus prays in the words of Psalm 36:6 a prayer of perfect trust in his Father: "Father, into your hands I commend my spirit" (23:46). With that, Jesus sets the direction for his "exodus"; according to Luke, his death will be a homecoming, the reward for his perfect humility and trust.

John's account of the passion is the most majestic of all. With supreme confidence, Jesus cries out, "It is finished" (19:30); his life is both coming to an end and is reaching the end for which he took it up in the first place. For John, Jesus is "the one sent" from God, and he returns to the Father only when his mission is accomplished. He has revealed in "signs" all that the Scriptures had hoped would come to pass and so he is triumphant, bowing his head in a deliberate act of humility and then "handing over" his spirit to the woman and the beloved disciple who, according to John, have been standing all this time as witnesses beside the cross. Through this Spirit (another "advocate") the work will go on—in the signs called sacraments of the church.

The gospel writers, then, tell the story of the suffering, death, and burial of Jesus in such a way that the significance of these events shines out in almost every detail. Within the Creed, their significance comes from their place in the story: they are the low point of the hero's "adventures": his going down into the grave where he grapples with the greatest of monsters, death itself. Only when he does battle can he claim victory, and that victory is proclaimed in the simple words that follow: "On the third day, he rose from the dead."

On the Third Day He Rose Again
in Fulfillment of the Scriptures

With the resurrection, the story of Jesus takes an upward turn, reversing the downward direction of suffering, death, and burial. With the ascension and the "sitting" in glory, the story shows Jesus in his proper element, completely in possession of his life's quest: life with the Father. For the Christian, this shows that the pattern of life is not ultimately downward to defeat but upward to victory because God can be trusted to be faithful. When God promises life, he gives life. "God will not," as St. Peter says, "let his holy one see corruption" (Acts 2:24–31).

The issue can be sharply stated: if the story of Jesus ends with the tomb, then life is, indeed, something in which there is much to be endured and little to be enjoyed. To say that Jesus suffered, died, and was buried is to tell a story that has often been told before, that life has a limit set by death, that the innocent as well as the guilty suffer and die with no hope of reward for their innocence, and that the point of life—if it has one at all—will have to be made up or arbitrarily chosen for oneself since there is no good to live for that is stronger than death.

These are the views of common sense, and many people have lived extraordinarily splendid lives according to these views. On the other hand, if the story of Jesus ends not with the tomb but with resurrection, then there is reason to hope that life has a direction and a purpose that are not merely made up and that cannot be frustrated even by death. To say "he rose from the dead" means that Jesus showed us not only the way to life when he spoke of the kingdom of God, but also that his way could be trusted to bring a person even through death to the goal for which life is given in the first place: life with God or, as it is called, "eternal life." But what does it mean to say that Jesus "rose" from the dead? What does "resurrection" itself mean?

For most people, the word suggests a resuscitated body, brought back to life with all of the needs, such as eating and sleeping, that pertain to a body. And then people have problems imagining what happens to the body after resurrection, how it could have ascended beyond the clouds and where it could possibly be. True, the gospel words taken in a literal sense seem to invite the imagination to picture resurrection and ascension like this, and the artists of the world have provided powerful paintings that encourage the imagination along these lines. However, such pictures, taken literally, create problems if a person were to ask how this kind of resurrected body would respond to laws of biology and physics from which no flesh-and-blood body can be exempted and still be human.

In other words, if Jesus' resurrected body were merely a refurbished version of his old body, how could he walk through doors—as Luke and John report—or how could he survive the change of air pressure in an upward ascent? I raise these objections of science in order to show that a poetic approach to resurrection is needed to grasp the meaning of the term. Pictures of what happened are helpful up to a point, but they cannot replace the point of the story itself. Just as "the map is not the territory," so too pictures or words that try to account for an experience are not the experience itself. In fact, they are especially sketchy maps indeed.

To discover what resurrection means, it helps to leave aside the pictures of a revived body and to ask what it means to say that Jesus rose "in fulfillment of the Scriptures." This phrase is one way of translating the Latin *secundum scripturas*, which can also be translated as "according to the Scriptures." This second translation is especially fruitful because it can be understood in three ways, each of which contributes a different emphasis.

In one sense, "according to the Scriptures" means nothing more than that the gospels and the entire New Testament testify to the resurrection as the end of the story of Jesus and that we are urged to believe this as good news. Our reason to believe such a startling turnabout rests on the testimony of witnesses. This reason is not enough to compel conviction, of course, but the testimony of the first witnesses also invites assent because for many hearers the story makes sense of the yearning for life. "According to the Scriptures," then, the resurrection is a fact announced by people who claim—with some credibility—to have witnessed it.

"According to the Scriptures" can also mean "in the way that the Scriptures say that he rose." Keeping in mind the accounts of the resurrection in the gospels and in the epistles, a person can see that the writers are trying to account in fumbling ways for an event that is both real and at the limits of their understanding and everyday experience. So, for example, Luke and John will say that Jesus had a body, and this seems to be affirming the real identity between the Jesus who lived once and who lives again (the risen Jesus is not a ghost). But they will also say that this body is not easily recognized, that it walks through doors, that it seems to come and go without hindrance. In other words, the risen body lives according to laws of its own.

In trying to grapple with this mystery for some very practical minded Corinthians, St. Paul came up with the idea of a "spiritual body," an apparently contradictory explanation that attempts to honor both the reality of the resurrection (that it concerns the human person who is, while alive, an *embodied* person) and the baffling dimension within which resurrection takes place. As Paul explains (1 Corinthians 15:35–38, 42–44):

> But someone may say, "How are the dead raised? With what kind of body will they come back?" You fool! What you sow is not brought to life unless it dies. And what you sow is not the body that is to be but a bare kernel of wheat, perhaps, or of some other kind; but God gives it a body as he chooses, and to each of the seeds, its own body....It is sown corruptible; it is raised incorruptible. It is sown dishonorable; it is raised glorious. It is sown weak; it is raised powerful. It is sown a natural body; it is raised a spiritual body. If there is a natural body, there is also a spiritual one.

According to the Scriptures, then, the resurrection of Jesus is a real event, but its reality is not exactly like anything else we know in our everyday lives.

Finally, Jesus rose "according to the Scriptures" in the sense that what he did was "in accordance with" or "in fulfillment" of those Scriptures. This is the deepest sense of the phrase because it means that the resurrection is to be seen as *the* point of the Scriptures (the Jewish Scriptures or Old Testament)—the only Scriptures known to the gospel writers. The resurrection is proclaimed as the key to understanding what God had been saying "in former times and in ages past" (Hebrews 1:1); it is the climax of a story that leads up to and away from this event.

A principal theme of the Jewish Scriptures is that God promises and gives land to his people. That is, God freely gives a great and tangible good to those who are faithful. Therefore, in order to understand at least one way in which the resurrection of Jesus fulfills the Scriptures, we should take a brief look at three key moments when God reveals himself to be the giver of the land. We will then see how in the resurrection of Jesus God brings the story to a climax by giving the "land"—the promised good—in a definitive and extraordinary way.

In the book of Genesis, in the very beginning, God brings the land out of water, the very image of an ordered world arising from a watery chaos. It is a place fit, it seems, for human habitation, a sign not only of power but of love that God should provide such a firm resting place for wonderful life.

Continuing the theme, God promises a land within the land for Abraham—the man of faith—and all his descendants who would be known as the people of Israel. Genesis traces the fulfillment of the promise of the land of Canaan from the promise to Abraham and Sarah, through its renewal to Isaac and Rebecca, and then to Jacob, Rachel, Leah, and their twelve sons. The great good of the promise of land remains with them as they migrate into Egypt to escape the famine where they live, and Genesis closes with the hint that the promise will soon be delivered.

The book of Exodus opens with the Israelites living in Egypt but under much harsher conditions than in Genesis. Over the years, the Jews become slaves of the Pharaohs and are put to work, building. But God does not forget the promise to the people; he sends Moses to lead them out of Egypt. They wander the desert of the Sinai peninsula for forty years while they learn the Law of God and prepare themselves for their new life in the land of promise. Through the leadership of Joshua, the successor of Moses, God gives the people the land of Canaan so often described as flowing with milk and honey (see, for example, Deuteronomy 6:3), and as they take up residence there they find life.

Unfortunately, after settling in Canaan, the people of God take their blessings for granted and begin to fall away from the faithful worship of God. According to prophets like Isaiah and Jeremiah, God demands justice and not mere lip service. If this is not to be their way of life, God will allow the people to taste how bitter their folly is. According to the Scriptures, God allows the people to be taken into exile—to lose the land. Once they realize what it really means to live in another world among other people, they long fervently for their homeland where they can once again be themselves. In time—a relatively short time, really—God sends hope to his people again by promising a return to their land through a second exodus that will outdo the first in splendor and joy.

This, then, is a key theme in the Jewish Scriptures: the giving of land as a promise after an exodus. If all of this is understood, it is clear why Luke refers to the passion and resurrection of Jesus as his "exodus." He is saying that Jesus enters into the great good that God the Father has promised to all who are faithful to him. Resurrection, then, means deliverance and vindication—an achievement of life that is far more vibrant than what can be experienced now.

Besides entering into this good himself, Jesus is like Moses, leading a people with him into the land of promise—if only they will follow him faithfully, united to him as closely as a body is united to its head.

And so the point of the story of Jesus—which is also our story—is that our lives are to be lived for God who promises life and gives it even in and beyond the suffering, death, and burial of all that looked like the only life there could be.

HE ASCENDED INTO HEAVEN

To say that Jesus ascended into heaven and is seated at the right hand of the Father is to draw out the message of the resurrection to its logical conclusion. Again, the imagination will want to picture what is happening for the sake of helping the mind fix its attention on something specific. Usually images from Luke's account in Acts 1:6–12 come to mind: Jesus' lifting his hands and making an ascent over the earth while his disciples look on until a cloud takes him from their sight. Such a literal picture is useful only if it helps to focus on Luke's real point: Jesus now belongs to the heavenly sphere of activity. This seems to be the point of the angels' question to the disciples as they stand dumbfounded on the mountain top: "Men of Galilee, why are you standing there looking at the sky? This Jesus who has been taken up from you into heaven will return in the same way as you have seen him going into heaven" (Acts 1:11). In other words, they are saying, "Jesus will return soon enough; meanwhile, don't you have some business to attend to? Has he not told you, for example, to bring the good news to all nations?" For Luke, the ascension of Jesus means that the time of Jesus on earth is over; the time of those who will continue his work has begun.

The author of Ephesians imagines the ascension in a way that is closer to the wording of the Creed and makes even clearer the point that the ascension marks the total victory of Jesus. Once he has said that the Father showed immeasurably great power in raising Jesus from the dead and in making him "sit at his right hand in the heavenly place," the author adds, "far above every principality, authority, power, and dominion, and every name that is named not only in this age but also in the one to come" (Ephesians 1:17–23). In other words, the ascension of Jesus means assuming the place and dignity that is rightly his: he is God's "right-hand man." To say this is to draw the logical conclusion that our loyalties are now best placed in him and not in any earthly power in preference to him.

As Paul reminded the Philippians, "our citizenship is in heaven" (3:20). This is what Jesus shows by sitting—fully human as he is—at the right hand of the Father, the place of honor at court. Jesus already is where the road of discipleship is leading. Believing this, our ancestors in faith knew that they could not place any loyalty above their loyalty to Jesus their Lord. That is why, when the Roman emperors demanded that they be given honors due to God, the early Christians knew that they would have to disobey the emperor to be loyal to Christ. They were punished with death itself as "disturbers of the peace," but the book of Revelation, which was written to comfort them, records the reason for their steadfast loyalty: Christ alone holds the key to everlasting life and shows us the "mystery" or "plan" of God for our salvation; he alone is worthy to receive "power and riches, wisdom and strength, honor and glory and blessing" (5:12).

To say that Jesus ascended, then, is to say that his authority as Lord is firmly established. To say that he will "come again in glory to judge the living and the dead" is to express the hope that God's just rule will govern earth as it already governs heaven. This is the Christian hope, that nothing will finally thwart God's plan for justice and peace.

The word "judge" may sound harsh to North American ears, but to the people of the Bible, judgment was a much desired good; it was the only way that justice could be done. To people who have lived without justice for a long time, the arrival of a just judge is a long-awaited event, a vindication for the long suffering under unjust oppression. The hope of the Scriptures is that Jesus will come as judge—liberator—of his people just as the judges of Jewish history did who arose in times of trouble: Samson, for example, Gideon, and Deborah.

Again, biblical authors picture the judgment differently. Matthew, for example, has the "son of Man" coming in glory and judging all nations like a shepherd who has come to separate sheep from goats. Paul pictures a trumpet call and the voice of an archangel announcing the coming of the Lord from heaven (1 Thessalonians 4:16). Revelation, in the most thundering image of all, imagines heaven open and a white horse appear; "its rider [is called] 'Faithful and True.' He judges and wages war in righteousness.... Out of his mouth [comes] a sharp sword to strike the nations. He will rule them with an iron rod, and he himself will tread out in the wine press the grapes of the fury and wrath of God the almighty" (19:11–15).

The idea behind all of these images is that our hope is to see Jesus again as the one in whose presence our lives will be sorted out and, if we have been faithful, will be found worthy of his company. Our hope is for the vindication of our service by someone whose glory is so impressive that it commands awe and obedience, even from his enemies. In a sense, that vindication is already available to those who submit their actions not merely to the standards of those around them but also to God's final judgment, which comes not with the blare of trumpets or the flashing of swords but most commonly in the quiet call of a well-formed conscience that has given in to God and has trusted God for the gift of that peace that no one can take away.

QUESTIONS FOR REFLECTION AND DISCUSSION

1. What is your favorite image of Jesus or story about him?

2. What experience of your own humanity do you think you share with Jesus?

3. In what ways is Jesus different from you?

4. As a person, the Virgin Mary is a powerful symbol; what does she signify for you?

5. How can you get closer to the mind and heart of Christ, and how do you know that you are getting there?

6. To what extent is a hope for "judgment" part of your life? How do you picture it?

7. What is your response to what you know of Jesus? What difference does knowing Jesus make to everything you do?

8. What images from advertising convey our society's judgment of what happiness or success is? How adequate are those words as poetic words? Do these words make the gospel words unnecessary?

9. What in our culture makes it hard to know Jesus or to make him more completely a part of life?

PART THREE

We believe in the Holy Spirit,
the Lord, the giver of life,
who proceeds from the Father and the Son.
With the Father and the Son
he is worshiped and glorified.
He has spoken through the Prophets.

THE GOSPEL WRITERS recall that Jesus promised to send his Spirit, and that he "breathed" his Spirit on his disciples after his resurrection in order to forgive their sins and—even more—in order to continue his story in their lives. *Spiritus* is the Latin word for "wind" or "breath" and signifies something that can be seen not in itself but in its effects. As a movement of air, wind may create violent or refreshing effects: as a tornado it topples buildings and trees, as a breeze it cools the brow. In either case it blows where it wills and is seen only in what it does.

To the Holy Spirit of Jesus is attributed all kinds of effects that lead to "life." For example, when the church of Corinth began to show unusual signs of "enthusiasm" (or signs of "the god within"), St. Paul agreed with the Corinthians that these were effects of the Spirit who was distributing different gifts to different people. Some people were getting up in the assembly and loudly praising God, even speaking ecstatically in strange tongues. From the very force of these outbursts, it seems, something was moving the Corinthians from within; like fans at a football game whose "spirit" is evident in their raucous cheering, the very quality of their breathing was forceful, even vehement. Their enthusiasm, or breath, argued to the presence of the "God" or the Spirit within. From the first, we can see, the church knew itself to be the people who breathe with the same breath as Jesus did; thanks to that Spirit, the church shares the mind of Christ, the life of Christ, and the very work of Christ in the world: the work of reconciliation and forgiveness.

St. Luke provides the best remembered account of how the first disciples came to feel the movement of the Spirit. The time is Pentecost, fifty days after Passover. Since Pentecost was a great pilgrimage feast, Jews were enjoined to go up to Jerusalem to celebrate it. So, as Luke describes it in Acts of the Apostles, Jews from all over the world were present in Jerusalem and the disciples of Jesus were also gathered together, praying in one room. They were frightened, aware that what had happened to Jesus— crucifixion and death—could very well happen to them.

Onto this scene, sudden and unexpected, comes the experience of something very much like the "rush of a mighty wind" and, with the wind, fire. In a poetic way, Luke describes what was an empirical fact: the experience by the first Christians of courage and conviction to go out into all the world and to proclaim with one voice (yet in many languages) that Jesus is Lord. The "breath of life" was the Spirit of God, and the power God gave was prophetic: the power "to speak on behalf of God."

The disciples soon recognized in themselves the same Spirit that had moved the great prophets of Israel from Moses to Daniel. Prophets like Isaiah, Amos, Hosea, and Jeremiah had spoken words of comfort and challenge on behalf of God to the people of Israel, and now the followers of Jesus were being prompted to do the same. Moreover, since they identified the hope held out to Israel with the life, death, and resurrection of Jesus, it could be said that the prophets (knowingly or not) had really but implicitly been speaking of the coming of Christ. To the extent that they had been offering a reason for hope, the prophets of Israel were really preparing the way during the centuries for "the One who is to come" (see Luke 7:20). Convinced, then, that the hope of the church and the hope of the prophets were really one hope (Jesus the Christ) and that the same Spirit that was moving the church had also moved the prophets of Israel, the gospel writers told the story of Jesus in such a way that echoes of the prophets' hope could be heard in his words and deeds.

St. Matthew is especially explicit about this, saying repeatedly that something was said or done by Jesus "to fulfill what was spoken through the prophets." The facts that Jesus was born in Bethlehem, lived in Nazareth, cured the sick, and entered Jerusalem in triumph are all told to underscore the point that the hope of the prophets finds its object in Jesus.

By giving hope to the prophets, the Spirit of God gave them an *implicit* knowledge of Christ; by "inspiring" the church with the awareness that Jesus is Lord, the same Spirit gave the church an *explicit* reason for faith, for hope, and for love. Because the Spirit can be credited with such effects, it is recognized as God's own Spirit and, with Father and Son, is "Lord."

The authors of the Creed take pains to stress the equal relationship of Father, Son, and Spirit precisely to emphasize that God is one God; at the same time, the church has come to know God only thanks to Jesus whose Spirit makes clear all that Jesus said and did. The Creed characterizes God as Father, Son, and Spirit in order to preserve the sense of the mystery: God is one without prejudice to diverse "persons" and lives a life that is as dynamic as it is diverse.

Because the influence of the Spirit can be extraordinary, the church has recognized two dangers from the beginning. The first difficulty is to distinguish one kind of spirit from another: the Spirit of God from the spirit of the evil one. In other words, enthusiasm can be exercised for good or ill. For example, when St. Paul persecuted the church he was "enthusiastic" for his work and went about, says St. Luke, "breathing murderous threats against the disciples of the Lord" (Acts 9:1). The "discerning of spirits" has to be done, then, according to some measure of faith. As St. John reminds his community, all spirits are to be "tested" in order "to see whether they belong to God" (1 John 4:1).

The second difficulty for the church is that the Spirit is the giver of divine life to people of various cultures, times, and places. There is always a tension, then, between the church of today and the church of tomorrow. At one time the Spirit inspires certain forms of devotion or communities of religious life; at another time, the Spirit retreats from these forms, it seems, and inspires others.

This has been so from the beginning, as Luke makes clear in a story from the tenth chapter of the Acts of the Apostles concerning Peter and the Roman centurion Cornelius. Having grown up a Jew, Peter and many others had strict ideas about what God expected in the way of keeping certain dietary laws and associating with non-Jewish, or Gentile, people. According to the book of Leviticus, there were such things as legally clean and unclean food and clean and unclean people. It never occurred to Peter that God might have something else in mind.

One day, in a dream, Peter saw a blanket let down from heaven in which every kind of animal was included—clean and unclean alike—and God told Peter to "slaughter and kill." When Peter objected because of his scruples over the dietary laws, God chided him, "What God has made clean, you are not to call profane" (10:15). After the dream, a Roman centurion, Cornelius, sent for Peter and asked him to come to his house so that he and his household could hear what Peter had to say. Thanks to the dream, Peter knew that he could not call this Gentile "unclean"— even though his training inclined him that way. When he arrived, Peter began to speak about Jesus as the one to whom "all the prophets bear witness," and as he did so, "the Holy Spirit fell upon all who listened to the word." As Luke reports, this was quite astonishing to the "circumcised believers" (the Jewish Christians) "that the gift of the Holy Spirit should have been poured out on the Gentiles also"—and yet, it was so. (See Acts 10:34 ff.)

The Spirit moves in disturbing ways at times, but thanks to the Spirit, life is given through faith to all peoples on earth. It is a life that shows itself primarily as conformity to Christ; the Spirit moves the disciple to act with the mind and in the manner of Christ. St Luke makes this point in an especially graphic way by describing the death of St. Stephen, in which the disciple is seen to be "another Christ" (see Acts 6:8–7:60). Stephen testifies to Jesus before a hostile audience and then is dragged to his execution. As he is being stoned, Stephen echoes Jesus' words of forgiveness for his enemies and then commends himself to Jesus, just as Jesus had commended himself to his Father (Acts 7:59 and Luke 23:46).

Paul identifies the life of the Spirit in Christ-like ways of acting. Paul is not impressed with esoteric gifts such as speaking in tongues or interpreting tongues, or even with prophecy or the working of miracles. These show an extraordinary inspiration of the Spirit, but the most Christ-like trait, the "more excellent way," is love, love that is for the other in so many ordinary and yet heroic ways:

Love is patient, love is kind. It is not jealous, [love] is not pompous, it is not inflated, it is not rude, it does not seek its own interests, it is not quick-tempered, it does not brood over injury, it does not rejoice over wrongdoing but rejoices with the truth. It bears all things, believes all things, hopes all things, endures all things (1 Corinthians 13:4–7).

Paul urged the Galatians (5:22) to acquire those virtues allied to love and calls them "fruits" of the Spirit's inspiration: joy, peace, patience, kindness, generosity, faithfulness, gentleness, and self-control. To Paul, it was a matter of a consistency in commitment. "If we live by the Spirit," he says, "let us also follow the Spirit. Let us not be conceited, provoking one another, envious of one another" (5:25–26). For Paul, the Christian life is not a matter of knowing more, or of having more, or of doing more, than someone else; it is a matter of being as closely conformed to Christ as possible by following the promptings of his Spirit.

Paul boldly urges us to trust that the wind that blows where it wills will bring us home if we but tack our sails to its direction.

Questions for Reflection and Discussion

1. What do you associate with "wind" or "breath"? How do these associations help you to understand "spirit" as it is used in the Bible?

2. What does it mean to be "prophetic"? How would you recognize a prophetic word today? Can you think of an example of a prophetic word?

3. Whom would you consider to be a prophetic person? How can you tell?

4. Some say that the Second Vatican Council was a movement of God's Spirit in our time; others would qualify that statement. What do you think is meant by calling something a "movement of God's Spirit," and how do you think such a movement could be confused with something else?

5. After you have reread St. Paul's words on love from 1 Corinthians 13, how would you compare these words with the way love is generally understood in our society?

6. In what ways does the church today show that it shares "the mind of Christ, the life of Christ, and the very work of Christ in the world: the work of reconciliation and forgiveness"?

7. What difference does it make to see the work of creating, saving, and sanctifying as the work of "one" God who is somehow also "three" persons?

PART FOUR

We believe in one holy catholic
and apostolic Church.
We acknowledge one baptism
for the forgiveness of sins.

FOR MOST PEOPLE who will read this book, the church is something of which they have direct experience; in fact, it is only through the church that they have come to know God, Jesus and the Holy Spirit. Starting with the family—the most local of churches—and moving out to the parish or other organizations, a person learns the story of God in ways that make it so much part of life that it sinks into the bones and runs along the nerves.

When the church convincingly mediates the mysteries of faith, it only makes sense for a person so convinced to admit that he or she believes or trusts the church. In one sense, then, to say that one believes the church is obvious. However, to say that one believes the church is "marked" as "one, holy, catholic and apostolic" is to say something far from obvious.

The Greek word for church, *ekklesia,* means "called out," and it refers to the people "called out" by God from darkness into light, from a shadow identity to a true identity, from sin to grace. As the first letter of Peter (2:10) puts it:

Once you were "no people"
but now you are God's people;
you "had not received mercy"
but now you have received mercy.

As the people of God, the church is a reality whose mystery is rooted in the call and the goal given to each baptized person. As a communion of the faithful, the church is at once all of the people who belong to Christ through faith and the sacraments, and the entire people, living and dead, who share the same call.

To speak of the church, then, is to refer to a variety of individuals with different gifts and ways of life who share a common vocation through baptism. They are to become like Christ in offering themselves to God, in witnessing to God in the world, and in advancing the reign of God in such a way that his will is "done on earth as it is in heaven." In traditional terms, the vocation is to become like Christ the priest, prophet, and king. It is obvious even to the casual observer that the faithful throughout history often fall short of their vocation. For this reason, the church's unity, holiness, catholicity, and apostolic identity are often obscure indeed.

It helps in moments of darkness to turn for light to some of the basics: the church is a people called—it is emphatically not a group that has banded together on its own initiative so that its rise and fall will depend on human wit and strength alone. Rather, the church is a work of the Holy Spirit much as St. Luke described it in Acts and as we saw in the last chapter. As a work of the Spirit, the church owes its very existence to "the Lord and giver of life" who gives the church a share in the very mind of Christ so that it can continue the story of Jesus in its members throughout the world and down through time.

As we saw in the last chapter, St. Paul reminded the church at Corinth that despite their varieties of gifts and despite their disputes about whose gifts were greatest, it was the Spirit of God who kept them one in professing their belief that Jesus was Lord, and who made them one in service of him (1 Corinthians 12:4–11). The work of the Spirit is unity, charity, and peace, and the church becomes what it is supposed to be when it responds faithfully to the prompting of the Spirit.

What the church is supposed to be has been described in various ways, but these symbolic descriptions are among the most powerful: the body of Christ and the bride of Christ. Logically, of course, the symbols should cancel each other out: one is male; the other, female. But as poetic descriptions they show different sides of a mystery that is bright with many facets.

As the body of Christ, the church is united to the Lord as the members of a body are united to the head. As one body, Christ and church live with the same life—the Spirit of Jesus is the Spirit of the church—and they share the same destiny as well. "Or are you unaware," as St. Paul reminds the Romans, "that we who were baptized into Christ Jesus were baptized into his death? We were buried with him through baptism into death, so that, just as

Christ was raised from the dead by the glory of the Father, we too might live in newness of life" (6:3–4).

In the gospel of John (12:26), this intimate union is expressed not only in terms of a vine and branches that share the same life-giving sap, but as a master and disciple who are to remain forever inseparable. Jesus prays before he dies, "Whoever serves me must follow me, and where I am there also will my servant be."

The church as body of Christ shares, too, in the dignity of Christ; if he is, in some sense, priest, prophet, and king, then the members of his body are also a priestly, prophetic, and kingly people.

As the "bride" of Christ, the church is imagined to be the well-beloved and chosen spouse of Christ. Like the bride of Isaiah's oracle, the church is God's "delight" (62:4). Like the bride in the Song of Songs, the church is called by the bridegroom, is wooed as lovely, and is united through love to her spouse. In cultures with a more male-centered understanding of marriage, the bride is seen as responsive and obedient to her husband who, in turn, is responsible for nourishing and providing for his wife. This is the understanding that lies behind the famous (and, to some, infamous) words of the letter to the Ephesians (5:22–27):

> For the husband is head of his wife just as Christ is head of the church, he himself the savior of the body. As the church is subordinate to Christ, so wives should be subordinate to their husbands in everything. Husbands, love your wives, even as Christ loved the church and handed himself over for her to sanctify her, cleansing her by the bath of water with the word, that he might present to himself the church in splendor, without spot or wrinkle or any such thing, that she might be holy and without blemish.

Because "subordination" between husband and wife in our culture does not respect the dignity of either spouse, the comparison of the church to a bride has troublesome connotations today. No one will disagree that the church owes obedience to Christ, but it does not help to try to strengthen the point by a comparison with the marriage relationships of Paul's time.

However this may be, St. Paul's emphasis falls on the self-giving love of Christ the wooer and husband and on the church as a radiant bride. One implication of the bride-groom analogy is especially fruitful: it shows how the church so often sees in the most earthy realities a hint of how God works in and through human life. If the church as bride is intimately one with Christ, it follows that precisely as the fruit of her union with Christ she will bring forth children who belong to the "family of God." The sexual union of husband and wife is a way of understanding not only the intimate and loving relationship between Christ and the church, but also the way the bride and wife becomes a mother.

This understanding of the church used to be enacted at the Easter Vigil when, at the blessing of the baptismal font, the priest would plunge the Paschal Candle, symbolizing Christ, three times into the "womb" of the font and would pray that the waters of the font in which the catechumens would soon be baptized might be made fruitful for the work of "regeneration." This ceremony shows graphically what the church is supposed to be: a people called by Christ and so intimately bound to him that it brings forth people who are like him and whose life is to be found in becoming more and more like their Lord.

Once it is understood that the church is in some sense "body" and "bride" of Christ, it follows that certain "marks" will distinguish the church's essential identity. And so we believe in the "one, holy, catholic, and apostolic" church as the church of Christ.

For example, if the church is "body" and "bride," then the church must also be "one" in order to embody the symbol effectively. After all, it would be unseemly if not blasphemous to imagine Christ with two bodies or a harem of brides. Unity is a hallmark of the church because there is only one Lord who requires only one faith (not two contradictory beliefs about himself) and who has commanded only one baptism with which to initiate all people into the mystery of that faith (see Ephesians 4:5). There will, indeed, be degrees of faith and different ways of understanding this faith, but those who are church will be one in faith as well as in charity and worship.

This is true, ideally speaking, but from the earliest days there have been dissensions within the church so fierce that they have showed all the more clearly how valuable unity is. Even St. Luke, who enjoys painting church life in the most ideal terms records a breakdown of unity almost from the start when Annas and his wife Sapphira try to keep some property for themselves after claiming that they have given all they own for the common good (see Acts 5). Selfishness shows itself from the start as dividing one from all.

Shortly after this, the rush of Greek-speaking Jews and then even Gentiles into the church threatens to divide those who believe that the commandments of Moses are binding on all who would be Christian from those who believe otherwise. The church restored unity in these cases through the authority of the Twelve working in concert with all the leaders, sometimes directly in council with them. Luke does not record that any broke from the unity of the church as a result of these crises, but no doubt many did. As in any age, change comes too slowly for some people, too fast for others. The difficult job is to find "the sense of the faithful" and to "feel with the church" in such a way that unity is maintained while change takes place—as it must—in all things but fundamental beliefs.

Although St. Luke does not record any "schism," or rending of the unity of the church, the gospel and the letters of John do allude to some severe divisions. Jesus prays at the Last Supper that his disciples may be "one" precisely because they are not united (John 17:11), and John's earlier reference to Jesus as the one shepherd who knows his own but who has other sheep "that do not belong to [his present] fold" also reflects the disunity of what used to be one community (see John 10:16). It seems that members of John's community differed over the identity of Jesus: was he merely human or was he also the pre-existent Word of God made flesh, the "one sent" by God? About such central matters there could be no compromise, and so groups broke communion with one another, each trusting its own belief to be the only creditable one. In some cases, one group found it necessary to deprive another group of communion with itself since common worship without common belief would be an empty ritual.

Even today, the Christian church is split into hundreds of "denominations" causing scandal for those who are looking for the "one" bride and body of Christ and finding all too often one group denouncing another as heretical and mistaken about what is meant by true belief.

Since the Second Vatican Council (1962–65), renewed efforts have been made among Christians to find again the essential things that unite them; to see if there does not exist a basis for unity despite different forms of worship and systems of church governance that have grown up in the four centuries since Luther took his "protestant" stand toward Rome and Rome excommunicated him. Protestants and Catholics are discovering a surprising amount of agreement over fundamental issues: the importance of the Bible; the role of Mary, the role of the pope in church life, and the meaning of the Mass. Nevertheless, lack of unity remains. This means that a person who would be Christian is faced with having to decide which of the churches most adequately embodies the unity and other marks of the church of Christ.

In this book my purpose is to explain a Creed that has been professed by Christians long before present-day divisions arose; I cannot try to resolve Christian disunity. However, the scandal of division must be mentioned and the search for unity must be maintained precisely because the church is the one body and bride of Christ. Schism and sectarian divisions maim the church, making it less responsive to its Lord and head and therefore less effective on his behalf in the world.

The church, then, is obviously not one, though to some degree it is. Likewise, the church is not obviously holy. It would be tedious, although honest to the facts of history, to list in detail the sins and scandals committed by people publicly identified with the church. In the *Inferno* of his *Divine Comedy,* Dante records the kinds of sin it is possible to commit in order of severity; on every level, he uses poetic license to place well-known examples of people from history, literature, and his own time who might aptly illustrate each sin. After reading the *Inferno,* a person has met all kinds of church people including popes, cardinals, and priests who have been found guilty, at least in the poet's eyes, of all kinds of sin. Dante did not blink at corruption, nor was he deceived by hypocritical appeals to blind loyalty in the name of religion. He told it like he thought it was, and it helps to remember that he wrote this "exposé" in the so-called Age of Faith—the late Middle Ages. Clearly, there never was a "golden age" of virtue; sin infects the church as well as the world so that the church must pray for forgiveness as much for itself as for others.

Of course, it is particularly scandalous when clergy and religious sin because it gives others even more excuse to go and do likewise. People reason that if all the high-sounding rhetoric about "repent and believe the good news" did not change even those who preached it, how can it be expected to convince those who are already skeptical?

The church was so scandalously wicked in Martin Luther's eyes that he thought it necessary to distinguish the visible church that was corrupt from the church of grace that was incorrupt and to call for a thoroughgoing reform of the visible church. The Catholic response to Luther was slow but sure; it instituted reforms through the Council of Trent but denied Luther's distinction between the two kinds of church. The Catholic response is to say that "what you see is what you get." The church is, indeed, imperfect as an institution and for that reason needs reform in every age. And yet since the church remains the body of Christ it cannot be completely moribund. The church remains holy in its head who is Christ, in its means of holiness such as the Scriptures and the sacraments, and in many of its members both living and dead who constitute a communion of saints. In other words, the church remains "marked" by holiness to the discerning eye even if it is hard to see holiness because of the sin that atrophies Christ-like action in many members.

History shows that there have been many cycles of corruption and renewal in the church, making it clear that what *has* been *can* be. Although there will be corruption, the church is also marked by a holiness that will flare out dramatically at times, even if it has been obscured for many years. In fact, the same Dante who showed so many church members as sinners in the *Inferno* shows in the *Purgatorio*, Canto 30, a vision of the church as a woman resplendent with glory, standing like a victor in a chariot drawn by Christ himself, who woos her with the words of Solomon's song, "Come from Lebanon, my bride" (Song of Songs 4:8). The church is surrounded by men representing all the books of the Bible and by women representing the great virtues of faith, hope, charity, prudence, justice, fortitude, and temperance. When the church speaks, her rebuke moves Dante to shame and repentance. Often, the church is obviously not a community of holiness—and yet to some degree holiness always is there.

Finally, the church is marked as catholic and apostolic, meaning that its message is the same as the apostles' preaching and that it is for all the world as Jesus said that it should be (see Matthew 28:18).

The Catholic church distinguishes itself by claiming that it holds fast to the preaching of the apostles recorded in the Scriptures and translated into documents such as the Creed we are studying now. Not everything the church says and does can be traced literally to the apostles. How could the apostles, for example, have made decisions about church government and worship that arose only as the church sought to function in cultures outside of the Palestine of 36 A.D.? How could the apostles have explicitly addressed questions of faith and morals that arose only when the church met challenges from different cultures and changing technology? In some ways, the church of today is not one that the apostles would immediately recognize—nor is the world, for that matter! Nowhere in the Scriptures, for example, does anyone use the word "pope," pray the rosary, speak about purgatory or indulgences, or even make the sign of the cross. Catholic practices and structures not directly found in the Scriptures are many.

Yet it is gratifying to think that if an apostle were to step inside a church and witness the celebration of the eucharist, he would soon recognize something quite familiar. Like the disciples on the road to Emmaeus, he would recognize Jesus in the breaking of the bread (see Luke 24:13–35). At the heart of the Mass is the apostolic practice of preaching the word and breaking the bread. If that same apostle were to ask about what had been happening to the church all these years, he would discover teachings and beliefs drawn by inference from the apostolic preaching in such a way that it would not be inconsistent with that preaching.

The church believes that its core faith and practices are apostolic in the sense that they do not contradict the faith of the apostles in an essential way. With that faith as its message, the church addresses all the world with the hope, as Pope John Paul II says, "that each person may be able to find Christ, in order that Christ may walk with each person the path of life, with the power of the truth about humanity and the world that is contained in the mystery of [his being with us in the flesh and redeeming us] and with the power of love that is radiated by the truth" (*Redemptor Hominis*, 13).

Because it is apostolic or "sent out" on mission, the church is also catholic, struggling to meet people of every culture, of every country, and of every walk of life with the amazing news of human worth in the light of the gospel and with the consequences for every sphere of human life that flows from that conviction of the God-given, inalienable worth of each person. The struggle, of course, is how to preserve unity of faith and charity in the midst of cultural diversity: how to be universal and local at the same time. This may seem an impossible goal at first, but it has been achieved before in sometimes simple ways; in its wisdom, the church has often integrated local customs (the use of incense) into its order of worship, and local heroes (St. George) into its communion of saints in order to ease the identification of any one people with all the people of God.

To be Catholic, then, is to live with the tension of trying to preserve two goods: the local flavor of life and the enduring truths that pertain to all life; one person's unique story and the one story of all people that threads its way through the Scriptures and is summed up in Christ.

The church is the work of "the Lord and giver of life" and is marked as "one, holy, catholic and apostolic." At times, its faults are so glaring that it belies its identity as the body and the bride of Christ. Yet the marks remain—however sadly concealed at times—so that someone with the mind of Christ or moved to acquire that mind, could understand how the author of Ephesians could say (Ephesians 5:25–27): "Christ loved the Church and handed himself over for her to sanctify her, cleansing her by the bath of water with the word, that he might present to himself the church in splendor, without spot or wrinkle or any such thing, that she might be holy and without blemish."

QUESTIONS FOR REFLECTION AND DISCUSSION

1. How have you come to know the church, and what are your feelings about it? What do you think about its claim to be the "people of God"?

2. In what way is each of the marks of the church evident in some local congregation like your own or one that you know?

3. For some people, the church is the strongest obstacle to their belief in God. Why might they think so?

4. If the church were to break up tomorrow, what difference would it make to the world?

5. What insights into the identity of the church are opened up for you by the comparison of "head" or "body"?

PART FIVE

We look for the resurrection of the dead,
and the life of the world to come.

THE CLOSING WORDS of the Creed hold out an object of hope that seems impossible to attain: "the resurrection of the dead and the life of the world to come." To common sense, the cycle of "ashes to ashes, dust to dust" gives a fitting shape to the human story. The body returns to the earth "whereto it is kin" and that ends the matter. There is some comfort in knowing that no one is exempt from going down into the grave—that by dying we can identify ourselves with all those who have gone before us, ratify the decree that "all this thing hath ende," make virtue out of necessity, achieve the peace that comes from being one with the unchanging order of things, or, in the poet's words, deliver ourselves to be "rolled round in earth's diurnal course,/ With rocks, and stones, and trees."

This ending to life seems not only fitting but also, to many, desirable. For those who have tired of dodging the "slings and arrows of outrageous fortune," death seems not only an end to life but also a deliverance from it, a well-deserved "rest" that should not be interrupted.

But after all has been said to adjust the mind to the fact of death, there arises in most people a disgust and even a horror that is in direct proportion to the evil of it. In one of the most famous icons of Western culture, Hamlet stands by the side of the grave and contemplates the skull of his father's jester, Yorick. He recalls the man's jests and gambols, the play of his mind and the movement of his body as he carried young Hamlet on his back around the court. Yorick told jokes once and set a whole palace into roars of laughter; now, there is only silence. As Hamlet says, "the gorge rises" at the thought of such things. It nauseates him to think of such life turned, finally, into such dust.

Despite the harsh conditions under which they often must live, people hope—absurdly, and even wistfully, it seems—for life. The Creed recognizes this hope and identifies it not as absurd but as a signal of life to come. With what reason can this hope be strengthened when to the common sense of so many people there is no clear evidence of any life after death? And, assuming there is reason to hope, what kind of life is there to hope for? Are we to imagine that billions of bodies will recompose themselves, for example,—that scattered ashes will be gathered together and that these refurbished people will find something to do—forever?

The Creed does not answer these questions directly, but rather leaves the believer free to find whatever explanations help the most. In this, the Creed is like a traveler's guide to a city. The guidebook will tell you what structure is there but not necessarily how it got there or even how the parts of the city all work together. To know the city's life more fully, you need history, politics, economic statistics, and so forth. Likewise, to know the Catholic faith, you need, beyond the Creed, a knowledge of the Scriptures, different theologies, and even canon law. So, the Creed points out that the "resurrection of the dead" is part of Catholic faith, but lying behind this is an assumption from Jewish belief that a person is nothing at all if not in the flesh. For the Jews, life can be seen by the breath that comes and goes, and when breath ceases, so does life. For quite some time in their history, there was no belief among Jews in any life after death. They held fiercely to their belief in one God; they kept alive his promise of the Land; they venerated their traditions and passed them on through the family as the only kind of "life" they had any reason to expect.

From the history of the Jews, it is clear that a belief in God can be held separately from any belief in a personal survival after death. If God gives life and then takes it away (by withdrawing the breath), what right does the person have to complain about that loss when he or she gratuitously received the gift of life in the first place?

Only late in Jewish history did the possibility of personal survival begin to dawn. The reasoning seems to follow from further reflection on the problem of evil. If God promises to uphold justice—to bless the just person and to curse the wicked—and if all people go down to the grave with the just unrewarded and the wicked unpunished, where is the justice? How is God to deliver on the promise if no one is alive to claim the promised reward?

The hope of heaven follows from the hope for justice. This is important to emphasize because some people have rejected the hope for "eternal life" or for "heaven" as a distraction from working for justice in the only life we know. However, heaven is no substitute for the justice that is denied on earth; rather, it undergirds the hope for justice here and now with the assurance that such a hope reflects an everlasting, undying cry of the human heart. If God is faithful and will uphold the claims of justice, then "heaven" is a way of saying that God's rule will prevail and will reward those who hunger and thirst for justice. The imagination may be baffled about how this is to happen; faith, however, is the assurance that it *will* happen.

Linking the hope for heaven with the claims of justice should distinguish the idea not only from wishful thinking but also from the frivolous images that have been attached to heaven over the years. Mark Twain, for example, took the symbolic language of the book of Revelation about people sitting on clouds, playing harps, and singing "Hosanna" behind pearly gates as a literal description of the activity of heaven. It was easy, then, for him to lampoon people who say that they hope to spend their "eternal life" doing this kind of thing while they don't seem especially diligent about putting in any practice time during the life they have here and now. Twain's satire strikes not only at the poverty of imagination that would picture heaven only in such terms but also at the hypocrisy of those who would say that they actually want to go to such a place.

The book of Revelation has provided only some faint images of what St. Paul said the mind has not pictured nor the heart even guessed. Clearly, then, it is a point of wisdom not only to learn to read symbolic language symbolically but also to seek out other, more helpful images of what is meant by "heaven."

In the course of the centuries, the church has used three images that have proven especially helpful and durable: rest, light, and home. In her liturgy for the dead, the church uses two of these images: "Eternal rest grant unto them, O Lord, and let perpetual light shine upon them." For quite some time, I used to think that the church was speaking euphemistically about death as a kind of sleep that came as a reward for all the waking and working hours of life. After years of hard labor, one could be grateful enough just for an end to it all, even if nothing more were to follow. However, it did strike me even early on that it would be hard to enjoy "eternal rest" if "perpetual light" were shining somewhere at the same time. Clearly, I had to think about what those words were saying if I were to make sense of them.

I broke the code when I discovered that the "rest" hoped for was a version of the same kind of rest that God enjoyed when, according to Genesis, God rested after six days of creation. The only thing God does on the seventh day is to "bless and sanctify" it precisely because it is a day of rest. It is a time to sit back, so to speak, and to look lovingly at everything that has been made and that is good. So on his day of rest, God is not sleeping; he is, instead, fully alert, enjoying the contemplation of that great good, the created world. The seventh day becomes the goal of the other six, since it marks a time of completion, the "end" toward which all of the activity is directed. Because "rest" is the goal of creation, it is used also in Psalm 95:11 as another name for the "promised land," the goal for the Jewish people after years of wandering in the desert. God's rest, then, is like a time and a place of complete satisfaction that consists of the enjoyment of goods that were constantly deferred in times of work and wandering.

Heaven is a place of rest, entered into by faith as the author of Hebrews explains (see Hebrews 4). It is a sharing in God's own act of knowing and loving the created world and, by extension, all that can be known and loved in the universe. It is not easy to picture how we will continue to know and to love in the rest that is promised to us. However, it is easy to believe that such a "state" of knowing and loving will not be boring. It is, in some sense, already reached every time a person has hung suspended in time, enjoying a movement of music or the glad moment of a child's smile. "Eternal rest" is the end of human life in the sense of its goal. Work is good, but not for its own sake. Work is for the sake of creating something that can, in turn, be contemplated and enjoyed in the time of leisure.

One of the lessons of this article of the Creed is that we are made for leisure, so that to lose the rhythm in which work is balanced by a day of rest is to lose something integral to our humanity. A society with no sense of leisure, because it is convinced only of the worth of work and consumption, will have no taste of heavenly activity either.

Since "eternal rest" means taking a long and loving look at the real, it is easy to understand why the church prays in her rites for the dead that "perpetual light" will shine on those who have died. Light cannot be looked at directly, but it is the means by which we can see everything else. The "light" of heaven is the means by which a person is able to see what is really there. So, in this sense Jesus is called the "light of the world." Wherever he shines, the truth is laid bare; wherever the shadows dissipate, sin and error slink away for shame.

In the *Divine Comedy*, Dante describes heaven as bathed in various degrees of light, all of it tempered to the degree that each soul is capable of enjoying God. There are varieties of light because there are varieties of people, all of them knowing and loving in a way that is unique and who would not lose their identities by being any different. The genius of Dante's presentation is to show at once the unity and the infinite variety of heaven; the souls are one in their knowledge and love of the same light, but they are unique in the manner and the degree of their response to that light.

Finally, heaven has been called the person's true "home." There is no intention of saying that the person literally had a previous existence in heaven to which one day he or she will return. Such is Platonic myth or Mormon belief but not the Catholic faith. Rather, heaven is "home" in the sense of a place where a person really belongs, and the time on earth is like a pilgrimage or a time of wandering before the "promised land" can be found. The image of "home" is meant to explain why it is that no good known on earth can satisfy a person for long. There is, it seems, in the human heart a restless desire to search for some good that is nameless and yet to be enjoyed. The Creed names that final good "the life of the world to come" and by offering it as the object of hope to the human heart the church confirms the fact that our hearts are restless, shows us the inevitable reason for this (that we are not home yet), and encourages us not to expect that any substitute good will satisfy us. If everlasting life, eternal rest, perpetual light is the goal, then it is wise to live in such a way that we will not feel out of our "element" when we have actually come home.

QUESTIONS FOR REFLECTION AND DISCUSSION

1. Is it made clear in our culture that work is for the sake of rest? If not, what is it said that work is for?

2. What would it mean to you to come "home"? Imagine this first as if you were a child, then a spouse, then a person living in a foreign land.

3. In what sense can it be said that heaven—and not earth—is the real home of humanity? What dangers lie in such an idea? What difference does it make to believe this or not?

4. Contemplation has been called a "long, loving look at the real." Can you recall a time when you have contemplated anything in that sense? If you have, how might that act be called a "heavenly" experience?

5. What do certain images of heaven such as angels with harps, clouds, and pearly gates communicate about the experience of heaven? Why do such images remain popular?

6. Some people object that belief in heaven is one way to take the injustices of this present life less seriously because they will be adjusted "later." How do you answer this objection?

7. Although it is hard to imagine an experience you have never had, how might you imagine the experience of heaven in such a way that it seems more "lively" and motivating?

Amen.

In THE COURSE of this book, I have paraphrased the words of the Creed to show how they make up a story and what the story is about. We have seen that, as poetic, the words of the Creed are "figured" or "turned aside" from everyday usage so that they say what they mean always in terms of something else. God is called "Father" and "Maker," for example, even though God has no sex and no hands, so that by means of these metaphors some enlightening perspective can be focused on human experience.

The story line of the Creed is also a way for making meaning clear; the truths of faith are arranged from the belief in the world as a creation through the drama of death and resurrection for the sake of salvation to the hope of the life that comes through sanctification. The shape of the story shows a purpose to its arrangement which, in turn, reflects the purpose seen in human life. However, the question may yet remain: granted that the Creed has something to say, what is gained by the use of poetic language?

As we have seen, poetry is an especially exact and intense use of language. In its ability to shed light on where we stand in life— on how it is with the human heart—poetry shines like lightning and not, as Mark Twain would remind us, like the lightning bug.

A poetic word like "father" says something so exact about God that something must be lost when the word is paraphrased. For example, if "our parent" were to replace "our Father," the personal and cultural expectations of "Father" and all of the emotions surrounding that word would be muted if not lost entirely. Like any metaphor or perspective on God, the word "Father" has limits to its effectiveness, but if the word were not to be used the perspective it opens up would never be enjoyed. Instead, a word with a narrower meaning or no word at all would take its place.

Poetic words are like limited but irreplaceable sources of light that make more or less adequate clearings in the darkness of our experience. The fact that each word is "only" a perspective does not diminish the fact that each word is also very much a perspective and should be valued for the help it gives a person to move forward on life's journey, even if only one step at a time.

It is the exactness of the poetic word, not the vagueness it is sometimes accused of having, that makes it so hard to understand at the same time that it is so irreplaceable and therefore valuable. As a poetic word, "father" has not only a dictionary meaning but also personal and cultural associations attached to it, and some of these are pertinent while others are not. In order to get the benefit of some associations the poet must risk the suggesting of others. He will use "father" in the hope of suggesting provident lawgiver, for example, and risk the fact that for some people the word suggests only abuse. Because the poetic word is exact, it requires the recovery of what the word could be said to mean in the context of the poet's culture and the recovery of the poetic structure in which it appears, and then the adding to these an emotional charge consistent with them from the reader's own experience.

To understand the words of the Creed, then, we have to recover the meanings they would have had in the culture of first-century Palestine and in the context of the stories of the Bible in which most of them appear. It should help to remember that these words were spoken with faith in an attempt to arouse faith; they were meant to mean something. Once we are given some hint of what that meaning could have been, each of us is faced with having to ask, "And what does it mean to me? Is my story reflected in that story? Is my heart stirred by the uncovering of the depth of my life known as 'God'"?

Clearly, it takes patience and courage to weigh the meaning of a poetic word and to understand it. It takes patience because picking up nuance and subtlety takes time and careful scrutiny; it takes courage, because poetic words carry a high emotional charge and suggest more than the reason is able to understand or to control. That is why in our culture where time is money or where television can solve even the thorniest of problems in 30 minutes minus commercials, sitting still to listen to the poetic word (even in church) is taken by many to be a waste of time. And where sophisticated technology has given the illusion that not much is or should long remain outside of human control, a truly overpowering word is at least a nuisance and at most a danger.

The culture we live in has its own reasons for resisting the gospels and the Creed. However, like the seed in Jesus' parable of the sower, the poetic word of the gospels and the Creed is broadcast for all to hear. It falls sometimes on the roadside, sometimes on thorns, and sometimes on rocky ground. Given the possibilities of rejection, it is a wonder that it ever falls sometimes on fertile soil where it yields a rich harvest.

In this book I have tried to improve the chances for the acceptance of this word by showing what kind of word it is and what human needs for meaning and purpose are satisifed by it. If I have succeeded, the reader can now say "Amen" to the Nicene Creed with more understanding and openess of heart. "Amen" means "Certainly," or "It is true," or "Yes, I believe." To say "Amen" to the story of the Nicene Creed is to say a word that puts the hearer into the story, changes that person from audience to actor, and unites the one person with the many who have ever said "Amen." It leaves the person at the point where he or she may enjoy the love of God made known by the Creed and where there is therefore nothing more to say.